The Art of
Raising Parents

The Art of Raising Parents
a young person's guide

George D. Durrant

BOOKCRAFT, INC.
Salt Lake City, Utah

Library of Congress Catalog Card Number: 77-87912
ISBN 0-88494-332-1

First Printing, 1977

Lithographed in the United States of America
Publishers Press
Salt Lake City. Utah

Contents

Chapter
1

Where
to
Begin

As I write this book, I can see my oldest son in my mind. He is a missionary in Japan. I really miss him. He is basically a really fine fellow. He's not as handsome as his father, but he's not bad-looking. He'll be even better looking when he returns from his mission, because missions make men more handsome. (I've been on two missions.)

Besides his looks, when he left he had other natural endowments. For instance, when he left home my family didn't have a year's supply of food; but as soon as he departed, we did have. It wasn't a miracle, exactly; it is just that I've never seen such a great eater as he was.

Before he went away I used to meet him for lunch at the cafeteria at Brigham Young University. He liked me so much that he'd wait for an hour if he had to, just for the privilege of eating with me (and perhaps for the privilege of giving me the privilege of paying the bill, which I always did). But now I go to the cafeteria and he's not there.

I go to the table where we used to sit and talk about his girl friends, his English class, basketball, and his feelings about religion and life. Now as I sit at the table again and eat alone, I smile and almost have to laugh out loud as I recall his funny stories — such as the one he told me about his mother and her credit card. It seems he accompanied his mother to a large local department store on that occasion. She told the lady in charge that we had just returned from a mission and we desired a new credit card. The lady seemed impressed until Matt whispered in a voice just loud enough for the lady to hear: "This is great, Mom. She's falling for your story. You just got out of the slammer for bad credit and she's going to give you a credit card." Needless to say, his mother had to do some fast talking.

Sometimes I sit there looking across the cafeteria and in my mind I see my son walking up to join me. This thought gets me very excited, but then I realize I'm daydreaming and I feel both sad and happy all in one thought.

I wish I could tell you how much I miss him, how much I love him, but I can't — words just won't do it.

It's like a story one of my missionaries once told me. This missionary had been quite an athlete. His father was his greatest fan.

One day this young man was in a crucial and exciting football game. With the score tied, only seconds remained before the final whistle. In an effort to win the game, the opposing team threw a long pass. The young man, a defensive back, leaped high into the air and speared the ball with one hand. He came down with the ball in his grasp and his feet in motion, outran the entire opposing team, and crossed the goal line as the game ended.

The fans went wild. The victorious team ran quickly to

the dressingroom. There was much jubilation there. The boy's father came in as his son was loosening his shoulder pads. The son shouted, "What did you think of that, Dad?"

The father tried to speak. His mouth opened but nothing came out. His eyes moistened. He stood there looking at his son with his weight first on one foot and then the other. And then, not knowing what else to do, he quickly reached into his back pocket, pulled out his wallet, opened it up, and plucked out his last five-dollar bill. He extended the bill to his son. The son took the money without even realizing what it was, and while he was looking down at it the father turned and was leaving. The son tried to call him back by shouting "Hey, Dad, I don't need this," but the father continued across the room and disappeared through the door. He had done the best he could to convey to his son his love and pride.

The missionary told me: "That was the only five dollars my dad had (I made him take it back that night). He was so proud of me that he couldn't even talk. That was an unforgettable day for me, because making a touchdown to win a game is a thrill of a lifetime. But that thrill was not as great as knowing that I had a dad who was so filled with love and pride for me that he couldn't even speak. After these many years that loving gesture from my father to me is my happiest memory."

How would you like a father like that — so proud of you he couldn't even speak, so he'd hand you a five-dollar bill? I can hear you now saying, "I'd really like that."

I told my second son the story that I've just related to you. He's an athlete. He said, "Dad, that kid really had a fine father." He then added, "How much would a winning basket in overtime be worth to you?"

I replied: "I'd use words instead of money. I'd say, 'I love you, my son.'" He replied, "I was afraid of that."

3

We fathers are all a bit different from each other. And so are mothers. We don't always know how to show it, but we all love our children. How do I know that all parents love their children? I know it because I know what's in my heart and I know that other fathers have the same kinds of feelings in their hearts. They feel as I feel. And so, speaking for all the fathers in the world, I say to you and all young people everywhere, "*We love you!*"

All parents make mistakes. They have their personal struggles. But they love you, their children. And when you are gone away, they miss you. They held you in their arms when you were a baby. They thrilled with your first word uttered as a child. They saw you take your first step. These things and a million others have caused you to be woven into their hearts so tightly that their love for you can never die.

Some parents can say "I love you" as easily as they can say "Hello." Others can say it with some difficulty. Others, because as children they heard it themselves so very seldom or not at all, can't seem to say it at all. Some parents show their love in many ways, others show it in a few ways, and some, because of their own problem, can't seem to show it at all.

Some of you know that your parents love you. Others of you strongly suspect that they do. And others of you really are a bit doubtful.

To those of you who know of your parents' love, I say, "You are most blessed, for there is no greater joy than to constantly feast on family love."

To those who strongly suspect your parents love you, I say: "You are correct. Build on that foundation and your life will be good."

To those who are doubtful that your parents love you, I say: "Please believe that they love you. Know that if it were possible to peel away all the hard shells built up by the trials of life and get to the true feelings of the heart, a deep love would be manifest there from them to you. The belief that they love you will be for you the beginning of your ability to love your own future children."

Yes, I miss my oldest son. There are thousands of young men and women on missions, but I deeply miss only one. And that's because that one is my son and I love him.

That's the way your parents feel about you. They love you. Only if you can feel that what I've said is true will reading on in this book make any sense to you. For it is only when you know that your parents love you that you can continue or begin the wonderful process and "the art of raising your parents"; raising them to heights that they could never achieve without your love and support.

By the way, I hope that when my son comes home he won't be as hard on the groceries; and, most of all, that he and I will be able to talk and laugh and be happy together as before.

Chapter
2

Some
Odd
Problems

Fathers and mothers are a little odd. Have you noticed that? I certainly have. As a matter of fact, the only people I know who are more odd than parents are the children of those parents.

Just what does "odd" mean? An odd-shaped orange is an orange that isn't perfect in shape. So odd people are simply people who aren't perfect. And since we hear the expression "Nobody's perfect," we can add, "so everybody's odd." I would accept that statement, except that I seem to be an exception. I'm one of the few people I know who isn't odd. And I'm sure that you are another one. It could be said that you and I are "nearly perfect." And if we can each quit lying we will be perfect.

My oldest son heard a joke once and he related it to me in a most serious manner. It went like this:

"I had a dream last night, and in my dream I died and went to heaven. When I got there, an angel met me. He led me to a room filled with what seemed to be millions of clocks. I asked him why there were so many clocks. The angel replied, 'There is a clock here for each person who is living upon the earth.'

"About that time I saw the big hand on one of the clocks suddenly jump forward five minutes. I asked, 'Why did the hand on that clock suddenly jump ahead?' The angel replied, 'Whenever the person on earth makes a mistake, his clock jumps ahead like that.' I then said to him, 'I'd like to see my father's clock.' "

By now I was spellbound by this intriguing story. My son's serious tone made me feel that he was indeed recounting an actual dream, and I was sure he was about to tell me something wonderful about myself. He continued:

"Upon my requesting to see your clock, Dad, he said: 'Your father's clock is in the next room. That room is rather warm, and we use your father's clock for a fan.' "

We were driving home from town at the time he told me of his alleged dream. It wasn't five minutes until I'd figured out what he'd said, and when I finally caught on I stopped the car and told him to get out and walk home. (He didn't, of course.) I wasn't able to look at a clock for the next several weeks without getting ticked off.

I suppose some of us would indeed be far ahead of our time if that dream was a reality. Do you agree, "fans"?

In this book I shall attempt to speak out of both sides of my mouth. I'll use one side to speak as a parent (I can do that because I am one) and I'll use the other side to speak as a youth (I can do that because I was one).

Speaking as a parent, I would like to announce that it's hard to be a perfect parent. It's especially hard to be a perfect parent if you have children. I have found that sons and daughters are the most difficult kinds of children to raise. Those kinds of children can make any parent a bit odd.

If your parents seem a little less or a lot less than perfect, you may well be a contributing factor. So try to understand and be tolerant and try to help them.

Study the following "untrue" case study. Only the facts and names have been changed:

As we look in on today's exciting episode in our story titled "One Boy's Family," we hear sixteen-year-old John, who has just finished his fifth piece of chicken, say, "We had an interesting discussion in my family relations class today."

"Oh," says Mother. "What about?"

"We were talking about today's parents, and we got on the subject of fathers," John replies as he licks his fingers. "We made a list that we felt describes the typical father of today."

At this point Father becomes more interested. John continues by pulling a paper from his shirt pocket and saying: "I copied the list down. I'll read it."

John reads, "Fathers are slightly overweight, particularly around the middle." Father quickly draws in his stomach muscles.

John continues, "Fathers often work too long, spend too little time with their family, and when they do come home they read a newspaper and don't talk to the family." Father gently folds the sports section of the evening paper that is resting in his lap.

John picks up a napkin and continues. "Fathers are often ornery and disagreeable." A pleasant but forced smile appears on Father's face, replacing the frown that John's earlier words had caused.

John reads on. "He spends too much time watching television and he doesn't read enough books."

Father suggests that John put the list away and do the dishes, but John reads on and on. "A father does not have as good a sense of humor as he ought to have. The hair on his head is not as thick as it used to be."

Father stands and announces, "On second thought *I'll* do the dishes."

As Father walks toward the sink, John seems to read louder. "He has the final answer to everything and doesn't want to listen to his teenage children's point of view. He wants to give orders around the home without explaining why."

Father returns to where John is sitting, snatches the paper from his hand, and says: "It's really gratifying to know that's the way fathers are. Is there anything good on that list?"

John replies, "No, we were going to list the 'good' things later, but this 'bad' list was so long that the class ended before we could get at the 'good' list."

A grin forms on John's face as he announces: "Now don't be upset, Dad. Half of those things on that list aren't even true about you."

"That's reassuring," Father replies in response to his son's gracious statement.

John continues: "You're a pretty good guy. It's just that you parents aren't quite as perfect as we young folks."

A large smile crosses John's face as he speaks again: "Dad, if you want me to, I'll work with you. You see, Dad, I like you even though you need a lot of help. I'm willing to help. I've got a feeling we can make a success of you sooner or later, and then you'll be as perfect as I am."

Father throws a dish towel at John and says, "If you really want to work with me, you can start by helping me with the dishes."

"There you go giving orders again," John replies.

And so ends the exciting case study. But as it does we are left wondering about these questions: Can perfect teenage John really help imperfect Father become perfect? And if he can help, will he? How will he do it? Stay tuned to this book for answers to these and other vital questions.

Which do you think would be the greater challenge, being a perfect parent or being a perfect teenager? Let's ask the question another way: Which is the more difficult role, being a parent or being a youth?

You are only guessing, because you don't know the answer. You've been a youth and you know that that is rough at times. But you've never been a parent. So you don't know of yourself which is the more difficult, do you? When you don't know the answer to a question, you should seek out an authority and ask him. An authority is someone who has written a book. I'm writing a book, so let's ask me. I shall now quote myself: "It is indeed difficult to be a parent, but it is *much more* difficult to be a youth."

I give that answer because my junior high and senior high years were very difficult for me — I wanted to be so many things that I couldn't quite seem to be. There was much frustration and heartache mixed with happiness and joy. Those were happy days but also difficult days. But I've said all that in another book, so I'll say no more on this matter except that for me it is easier being a parent than it was being a youth.

Let me quickly add, however, that being a parent is almost as difficult as being a youth. And furthermore, striving to be a *good* parent is among the most difficult of all tasks.

Now let me talk out of the teenage side of my mouth. You're probably a bit like I was. (Perhaps not as handsome.) You and I are more alike than we are different. The feelings of the heart are about the same for all of us.

I struggled as a young person, and I believe you do too. The question is, can you in your struggles and frustration and moodiness and orneriness and feelings of inferiority help your parents with their struggles and frustrations and moodiness and orneriness and feelings of inferiority? Of course you can. We all know coaches who can't even run but who can help others be all-American. If we can transpose that concept into the Church scene, that's what this book is all about — making "all-Family" parents out of your mom and dad.

If your home is not a happy place now, you have a responsibility to make it so. And if it is already a happy place, then you have an everlasting responsibility to keep it that way.

It's sad to consider, but many families have really fallen apart. Perhaps you feel that such is the case in your home. If so, you can and must do something about it.

Most likely you, my readers, are members of the Church. But many of you have fathers or mothers or both who are not members. Many of you have parents who are members but who drink or have other problems. Others of you have fathers who go to church but who are not as pleasant around home as they could be. There are some of you whose parents don't seem to get along together, who seem to criticize and act hateful toward one another. Some of you come from homes where you sense a negative atmosphere.

In other words, some of you really have a big challenge. Life is filled with challenges. In the preexistence, before we came to earth, we agreed that we'd welcome challenges. Life is not an easy ball game. The opposite team is led by a devilishly good coach. But those who have played ball welcome a tough opponent. It's no fun to be in a dressing room lacing up your shoes when you know that tonight's game is against a team that has lost sixty-nine straight games. You hardly even want to play them.

But on a night when the best team in the state, the undefeated champions, are coming to town to play you, that is when you can't wait to get at them. That's when you say: "We'll win! We've got them on our floor with our referees and we're going to beat them." You'll have to decide, considering your family, just how tough the game will be at your home. But you've got the home court advantage and the great Referee is on your side. So get in there and do it.

I know you have problems of your own. You feel like a sub sitting on the bench. You feel as though it would take a star to pull off such a victory. I recall once sitting on the bench in a vital basketball game. I usually didn't enter the game until the score was 87 to 24. (It didn't matter who was 87 or who was 24.) But this night our main center fouled out with more than a full quarter to go. The coach was panicky as he looked down the bench at me. He stalled; he insisted they count the fouls again to see if our star really did have five. But finally he had to do it. He had to put me in.

As I took off my warm-up jacket, my cousin, who was a city policeman, came down to where I was. He said to me: "Get in there and play. Don't you embarrass our family." That really made me feel good!

I entered the game. We were playing against last year's state champions and the score was tied. The challenge was great for me and I found myself wishing I could be a star.

I'd say more about the game, but this is a deep philosophical book, not a cheap sports page. All I really need to say is that foul pitches count one point and I made one foul pitch and we won by one point. There, that night, I found out that all it takes to make a sub into a star is a chance and a challenge and just one point.

So get up off your ornery inferior self-pitying bench and get in there and become a star. Lift your parents up on your shoulders. You may not make all-American, but think of the honor if you are named "all-Family"!

Chapter

3

Take Five

While I was growing up, my mother would awaken me on Sunday mornings. I would get out of bed, because I knew Mother expected me to, and I'd hurry off to priesthood meeting.

One Sunday morning when my mother called me, however, I quickly turned over and tried to go back to sleep. In a while she came back and said, "Aren't you going to priesthood meeting?"

Now, I wanted to honor her desires, and normally I would have, because I was a good fellow; but, you see, I was really tired that morning and sleep seemed to be a bit more important than honoring my mother. So I didn't reply to her question.

"Are you asleep?" she asked. Again I didn't reply.

Finally, warmly and lovingly she pleaded, "George, please get up and go to priesthood meeting."

I opened my eyes and looked at her; in fact, I almost

arose, but then my head fell back down on the pillow and I acted as though I had gone back to sleep. My mother then left me alone. I knew I had hurt her, and that worried me so much that it took me several minutes to go back to sleep. But then I slept through priesthood meeting and Sunday School.

That day when I appeared at the dinner table I felt like an unwelcome guest. My mother didn't refuse to serve me, but her heart wasn't in it. She let me know just by the expression on her face that she was deeply disappointed and to a degree heartbroken that her son had not attended priesthood meeting. That was not a pleasant Sunday dinner for me. The food was just as good, but it didn't taste as delicious as usual.

The next Sunday morning she called me again: "George, it's time to get up for priesthood meeting." (She never did give up on me.) I remembered the week before. I was sleepy this morning too, but I didn't want the misery of hurting my mom again, so at her call I bounded from the bed and was off to priesthood meeting. I recall coming home that day and devouring one of her delicious dinners. This time I could tell that her heart was in it. "Be sure and eat plenty of the chicken and noodles," she said. She was so glad to see me after I had been off to my meetings, because that meant I was growing up to be a full member of the Church. I loved chicken and noodles, and the more I ate the more I felt like a full brother.

That's the way it always went for me. I could disobey my parents. I could "sleep in" in the morning, "stay out" in the night. In numerous other matters I could have my own way. But when my way was contrary to their way, I went toward misery rather than happiness. Whenever I failed to honor my parents, that certain something that made me feel right just wasn't there.

During family home evening, a certain family was discussing the Ten Commandments. The father asked each family member to choose from those Commandments the one which he or she thought was the most important. After making a choice, each of the family was to tell which of the Ten Commandments he had selected. Fourteen-year-old Ross awaited his turn, then announced that the commandment which he had chosen was the fifth one: Honor thy father and thy mother.

When each had told the family the commandment he had chosen, the father said, "Now, each of you take the commandment you have suggested and try to completely obey that law for one week."

As Ross heard this challenge, he felt that he had made a poor choice of commandments. He was almost panicky. "I want to change my commandment," he said.

"All right, Ross," his father said, "which one would you like to change to?"

Ross quickly said, "I want to change to 'Thou shalt not kill.' "

Father let him get away with this and Ross relaxed, sat back and smiled. He felt that he could handle "Thou shalt not kill," but to "honor his parents" for a week was too great a challenge. As with Ross, I'm sure that to many of you it seems at times that it would be much easier to keep any of the other commandments than it would to *truly honor your father and mother.*

It seems it would be easy to honor them if they'd say:

"Whatever you say, son."

"Come home when you choose."

"The way you look is your business, not mine."

"The car is yours anytime you want."

"Just tell me what you want and we'll get it for you."

"I'll clean your room."

"It's not your fault."

"It's your life."

And if they just wouldn't say:

"Because I said so, that's why."

"Because no child of mine is going to have hair that long."

"Because those grades are too low."

"Because it is good for you, that's why."

Or:

"When I get home, it had better be done."

"Ten-thirty and no later."

"You never get your homework done."

"Your room is filthy."

"Stand up straight."

"No more TV tonight."

"Eat everything on your plate."

"Get up."

"Go to bed."

But if your parents said only those things in the first list and not the things in the other two lists, it would be like an umpire not saying "ball" or "strike" but instead saying: "I don't know if it was high or low or just right. Why don't you just decide. Whatever you want, Mr. Batter and Mr. Pitcher, is all right with me."

It is your parents' duty to call "balls" and "strikes" and "outs" and "safes." Ball games with umpires who call everyone "safe" would soon become dangerous places to be.

At times when we parents seem a bit demanding and when you wish we'd ease up a bit, you should consider the great demands the Lord places on us. There are not many people anywhere in the world who are trying to get their children to do what we parents in the Lord's Church are trying to get our children to do. Latter-day Saint parents are taught by the scriptures that it's our duty to bring up our children in the Lord. He has told us that if we don't teach our children the gospel by the time they're eight, then the sin will be upon our heads. Thus the Lord clearly commands mothers and fathers that we must teach our children.

You can understand, then, that we parents are under considerable pressure. If we see you, our children, doing something which we consider wrong or likely to lead to wrong — your hair getting longer than we think is appropriate, or your dress not being as long as we feel it should be, or staying out too late, or any one of a number of things — we think you may be going downhill. We begin to be concerned about whether you're going to do the things the Lord expects of you.

When children in other religions smoke, it's usually no big crisis in the eyes of their parents. When young men in other churches turn nineteen years old, there's no pressure upon their parents to have produced a boy who wants to go on a mission. There's no pressure on other parents to see that when their children are ready to get married they are living in such a way that they're worthy to get a temple recommend. No other parents are expected to raise children who will pay 10 percent of their income as tithing. But all these things and more are expected of an LDS parent. In the Church we place great emphasis too upon getting a college education or going to a trade school. Our standards are the most lofty of any society in the world.

Naturally, sometimes we parents get a bit nervous about the situation. We want to be obedient to the Lord's will and to be good members of the Church, and we feel that as such our number one duty is to succeed in raising righteous children. To succeed in that way we feel that we have to have a rather tight rein on you. You should understand this divine pressure that comes to us through the holy prophets. When you come to realize that being a parent in the Church is not easy, that it's almost as difficult as being a youth, then perhaps you'll have more compassion for us imperfect moms and dads.

To make it more difficult, not many of us parents have complete tact and perfect wisdom in knowing just how to carry out the difficult assignment of parenthood. But you can rest assured that one of the reasons we want you to be special is that we are trying to do the will of the Lord. And you can't really criticize us for that. What we are trying to do is right. It's just that sometimes we can't seem to do it just right.

And when we parents make errors in the way we handle our task and you rebel, we really have a problem. It's like cows in a pasture. Somebody has said that if you put a fence around a pasture, the cows will want to push against the wire, push against it, and push against it some more. They continually try to get the grass that is just barely on the other side of the wire.

Now, some young people are like cows in this respect — they see rules or parental requests as a fence that is holding them in. For that reason they push against family standards in a constant effort to reach something just beyond the fence. All that that causes is higher, tighter, and more numerous fences. The best thing a young person can do is graze the middle of the field. Just try to live in such a way that we parents know that you're trying to do the right thing. That lets us parents relax a little more. Living with righteously relaxed parents is a real joy. When both you and they are relaxed, you can talk with each other and enjoy life together.

I talked to a judge one day. He said, "The trouble with Mormon parents is that they try too hard." I replied,

"Judge, you are wrong." (I said that once before to a judge, but I still had to pay him twenty-five dollars.) I went on: "They don't try too hard. Parents can't try too hard. It's just that they try the wrong things too hard." You can help your parents relax by grazing in the middle of the field. Then they can do something that is much better than building more, higher, and tighter fences.

If life is a continual crisis, with your parents always wanting to build closer, higher, stronger fences by issuing ultimatums, and you trying to go beyond those fences, then life really can become miserable — both for you and for your mother and father. And under those circumstances the judge might have a point.

There's probably no situation in which rules will be created faster than when we parents detect that you're rebelling. Most parents just naturally feel that the only way to solve a problem with their children is to create a new rule. Those rules become harder and harder to keep, and that leads to more rebellion and a need for more rules, and soon the young person must either obey hundreds of rules or else rebel. The solution is to stay in the center of the "field." Then it's almost as if there are no rules at all. All that then controls you are words such as *honor, trust, love,* and *respect*. I like all those words better than words like *rules* and *fences*.

I know one young fellow who was quite well fenced in as a youngster, but as he got older he began to push against every rule his parents had made. Each time he did this they would bring him back by sheer force. They were larger then than he was and had control over him. But finally he grew to be so large that they couldn't tell him what to do any more. They'd used all the force and fear on him they could use and they had nothing left in reserve. As a result, he pretty well ran a bulldozer through all their fences. In doing so he broke his parents' hearts and nearly destroyed himself. Whose fault was it? For our purposes it doesn't matter whose fault it was. The thing that matters is *you*. There is still time for you.

What are you really doing if you rebel against your parents when they are trying to do the right thing? You are moving into the area of wickedness. Obviously, if your parents are trying to teach you righteousness and you disregard their teachings, then you certainly are not standing on righteous ground. And when you stand on wicked ground you are miserable, because the Lord has clearly taught us that "wickedness never was happiness."

While I served as a mission president in a distant part of the land I talked to a fellow who told me some of the things he had been doing in the way of rebellion. He had smoked, drunk, used drugs. And through it all he had come and gone at will. He had broken his father's heart.

I ventured a question to him. "How does it make you feel to know the great sorrow which you've brought your father and mother?"

He started to cry and said he hadn't really wanted to do that. "I just felt that it was my life — not theirs," he said. He now seemed heartbroken as he realized the deep sorrow he had caused his parents. I detected that he was sincere. I counseled him that he should repent and go and try to mend the fences. He said it would be hard. I agreed that it would be hard but insisted that he should do it. He has his agency to go on rebelling, but with him so miserable and his parents so miserable it just didn't make sense to continue in that way.

At a certain age you can of course decide that you won't go down the road your parents desire you to follow. We all know that there comes a time when the young person can do just about what he or she decides to do. To those of you who decide to not honor your parents, I would suggest that you at least be kind to them and strive to think of them. As you begin to break their hearts (and you will, you know), be as gentle as you can. Let them know that you love them but that you've decided not to go the way they want you to go. Tell them that you've chosen to go your own way but that it's not their fault. Let them know where you will be, so that they will not have to lie awake at nights worrying about you, wondering where you are and what you are doing.

We parents have many concerns. A father might lose his job; the income may not stretch sufficiently; or any one or combination of dozens of other difficulties may be matters of daily concern and worry to parents (and usually their children will not be aware of them). But the greatest problem that can beset parents is for their children to disregard their counsel and go out and openly rebel. For a father and mother to wonder where their rebellious son or daughter is, or to wonder what he or she is doing, is one of the greatest pains a parent can have. I don't suppose there's ever been a more cruel form of punishment devised by man than the suffering parents experience when their children refuse to honor them by turning their backs on their family and on their God.

To those of you who choose to rebel against righteous parents, I venture this bit of moralizing. "Someday when you have children of your own, you'll know how much you made your parents suffer; because then you'll know that all that they long for and dream for and work for is for you." So please be kind to them.

Perhaps I should emphasize here that honoring your parents doesn't mean that you have to obey them when their requests would take you away from the principles which you know are true. There are times when parents might suggest actions that would lead a son or daughter away from rather than toward the Lord. On those occasions that son or daughter would need to use great wisdom. I saw a small but exact example of this at a baseball game, where a father passed his cigar to his little son. His son put it in his own mouth, struck a match, and lit the cigar. After the cigar was going, the son passed it back to the father. Certainly this is not what is meant by honoring parents.

I knew a missionary once who was afraid to return home after his mission because he feared his parents would lead him into a sin-filled life. In order to join the Church he had had to break his ties with them; and he feared that if he went home he would not be able to remain true to the Church.

This missionary did return home. He was right in his apprehensions — his family enticed him to alcohol and drugs and he fell. He has now left home again in the hope of rebuilding his shattered life.

If you are one who must face unrighteous parents, remember that the Lord will help you. Your greatest desire should be to so live as to be certain that your children will never have to suffer what you have suffered.

I knew a young man who came to Brigham Young University because of the strong program it offered in his field of study. Being a non-Mormon, at first he didn't want anything to do with the Latter-day Saints' religion. But as he heard more in his Book of Mormon class and in his branch, he became interested. He began to pray. There came to him an overwhelming testimony that the Church was true and he decided to be baptized. His father was not sold on the idea, but he did say that he would not object if that was his son's desire. The young man therefore got baptized, and as the semester went on he became more and more thrilled with the Church.

At Christmastime he came to me. "I won't be back," he said. "I'm going home because I want to be with my parents. They need the gospel just as I needed it and I'm going home to see if I can bring it to them." He added: "I'm going home because my dad's a great man and my mother's a great woman. I'm going home to live in their house and work and go to school there because I want to help them."

Then he said: "Pray for me, because it's going to be hard to be at home. They don't see things as I see them. There are many things that they like to do that I wasn't in favor of when I went away, and now I'm far less in favor of them." He was willing to get up off the bench and enter a most difficult but crucial game. I'm praying now that he will be a "star" that will lead his parents to the truth.

Every one of us has his own set of circumstances in relation to the fifth commandment. But interwoven into each of our lives is the basic truth which says, "Honor thy father and thy mother." That is the standard for each of us. Fit it into your life in the proper way and you'll be happy. Bring honor to your parents by loving them, respecting them, and obeying their righteous requests, even if those requests are not always perfectly, tactfully, appropriately, lovingly made. Remember "nobody's perfect" — except you and me.

Ross, you recall, wanted to change his commandment from "Honor thy father and thy mother" to "Thou shalt not kill," for he felt, and correctly so, that this second choice would be easier to obey than the first. But who wants an easy way? That's like playing against a loser. So you win?

So what? But of all the commandments given, there is not one that opens a potentially more difficult door but which leads to a more glorious area of happiness than that which says, "Honor thy father and thy mother."

Chapter
4

Use
Parent
Psychology

In books which parents read about how to help their children there is often much material that could be categorized as "child psychology." Isn't it only fair, then, that as young people consider how they can help their parents something should be said about "parent psychology"? The approach of this book is that in order to change negative aspects of family life you must initiate positive action. If there's going to be a truly happy relationship between you and your parents, you're going to have to cause it to happen. "Parent psychology" is one way to bring about such changes.

While I was growing up, some people said my mother did too much for me. I recall many people saying to her, "You're spoiling him." When I'd hear that, I'd think: "Why don't you mind your own business? I don't mind being spoiled." When I'd come home from school, my mother was almost always there. She'd immediately ask me if I wanted something to eat. And I'd always say yes. Then she would get out the bread and the butter and the peanut butter and make me a nice piece of bread and peanut butter.

Sometimes while she was concocting this delicious creation someone else would be watching. That person might say something like: "What's the matter with him, has he got a broken arm? Why don't you let him make that himself?" My mother wouldn't reply; she'd just go on making the sandwich. As long as anybody was there I wouldn't say anything either. But when the person had gone and just Mother and I were there alone, I would say to her, "The reason I like you to make me peanut butter and bread is that when you make it, Mom, it tastes better." When I'd say that she'd smile and look at me with love in her eyes and say, "George, I'll just keep on making peanut butter sandwiches for you as long as you want me to."

Yes, I suppose my mother did spoil me. But I sort of spoiled her too. I used a lot of parent psychology on her. But let me point out that none of the parent psychology I used on my mother was ever insincere. I never told a greater truth than when I told her, "When you make it, it tastes better." It was just something about the way she did it. I never ate a meal at her table that didn't taste like a banquet. It was just simple food, but when Mother set her hands to something it was magnificent. So what was wrong with telling her so?

I used to leave my mother notes telling her how much I loved her. And I noticed that when I did such things she was all the more anxious to be with me and be my friend. My mother really did spoil me. She didn't have any money or any *things* she could spoil me with, she just spoiled me with her love. (Here let me say something to all you mothers who might read this book: you go right ahead and spoil your children with love.)

I once heard an old fable that can be used to portray the way parent psychology works. In the fable the sun and the wind were discussing which one of them was the stronger. Each claimed to be the most powerful force in the universe. Finally they agreed to a contest. They looked down upon the earth and saw a man walking along a road wearing a coat. The sun suggested that each of them try to get the man's coat off.

The wind agreed to make the first attempt. He began to blow, starting out with soft breezes and gradually increasing them to fierce gusts of cold air. After a while the man buttoned his coat; then as the gusts increased in intensity he held it tighter and tighter around him. After using all the force he could muster, without success, the wind finally gave up.

Now the sun took his turn. He came out from behind a cloud and slowly began to warm the earth. Soon the man relaxed his grip on the coat. Then he unfastened a few of the buttons. After a while he took his coat off and carried it on his arm. The warmth of the sun had accomplished what the harshness of the wind could not do.

If you treat your parents negatively, sarcastically, or complainingly, you will be acting as the wind does — you will not help them at all. Such an attitude will make them feel tense and pressured. But if you use warmth, love, and consideration, you will find that you will have great power in blessing the lives of your parents. If you do these things sincerely, not as a means of manipulating your parents but just to show appreciation, you will do wonders for your relationship with them.

Once when I talked to a friend of mine who has six

children, he told me of a special experience he had recently had with one of them. He had taken the family camping for a few days and had really tried to make it a wonderful time for them. When it came time to go home, all of the children were away from the camp, playing and generally having fun. My friend was putting everything away and getting ready to go, and as he got down on one knee to hitch the trailer to the car, he noticed one small son running up to him. In recounting that experience, he said: "Little David just came up to me and put his arms around my neck and said: 'Dad, thanks for bringing me! I had fun. You're a neat Daddy!' " And as my friend said these words, he teared up and choked a little.

The reason that meant so much to him is that it isn't easy to take the family camping. It isn't easy to do a lot of things for the family. But, as my friend told me then, "Just that one moment of sincere appreciation was worth any effort I put into the trip."

Think about it for a minute. Consider these words: "You did a good job." "I appreciate the effort you made." "You are really a neat person." How does it make you feel when someone says such things to you? Very few people can keep going day after day, doing things that are hard to do, unless they get some appreciation in return. Your parents have that need. You ought to let them know they are appreciated.

Yes, you can use psychology on your parents, but not to manipulate them. You don't want to take advantage of them. You just want to do those things that will cause your parents to behave in such a way that you can get along with them and they with you.

As an example of parent psychology, an ornery father can be changed to a pleasant father by a kiss on the cheek

30

from his pretty teenage daughter. If you girls don't think so, just try it some time.

As for you young men, a father can be brought into some stimulating physical activity by a teenage son who says, "Shake on it, Dad," and then grips his father's hand in a way that makes the nervous system know it's alive. If you do that, your father will want to grip too. He'll say something like: "Let me have an equal chance. I didn't know you were going to grip my hand. Let's try that again and we'll see who's got the strongest grip."

So you grip again and your father grimaces again. Then he says: "So what, so you've got strong hands, what does that have to do with anything? Do you want to have an arm wrestle?" Then you can have an arm wrestle with him. Then he'll find out he's not as tired as he thought he was. There he is engaging in some sports events with you. Through parent psychology you've encouraged him into some things that can bring good father-and-son re-lationships.

Good parent psychology demands that you treat your parents with respect and love. If you do that, they will just seem to be compelled to respond in the same way.

Using sincere compliments is good parent psychology. I recall a conversation with my daughter. She said to me: "Dad, the guy I'm going to marry is going to be really something. He's going to be handsome. He's going to be good. He's going to have a great personality. He's going to be really religious and a leader in the Church. He's going to be talented." After several more descriptions of the perfect man, she said, as she put her hand on my shoulder and looked into my eyes, "He's going to be just like you, Dad."

This message came to me at a time when I felt a little bit discouraged and a little like a failure — and most of us feel that way at times. Those well-timed words filled me with hope; and, oh, how they filled me with love for my daughter! Just the fact that she would say something like that about me really touched me. As a parent I know how much we need to have our children tell us sometimes that they think we are good parents.

One boy told his father something that the father considered to be the greatest compliment he had ever had. This boy had had some bitter disappointments and was in the depths of discouragement. Feeling that he wasn't making it, he was even talking about quitting school and thinking of other negative actions. The father went to his son's room and the two of them had a long visit.

Because of the talk they had together, the boy started to feel better. As they continued talking, almost with an emotional outburst the son said to his father: "I know I can still make it because I've got the perfect example to follow. I've got you, Dad, and I want to be like you."

The father told me that he couldn't hold back the tears when he heard this. His son had not said anything like that to him in years. As he looked at his son on that occasion, he felt that he had the finest son who had ever lived. That single expression from his son did more to cement the relationship between the two of them than anything that had happened in a long time.

Of course, you can't say things like that if you don't mean them. But there are times when there surges into your soul a feeling of great love and admiration for your father or your mother, and you simply must tell them. If you can't tell them face to face, tell them in a note. Let them know of your appreciation. This will unlock a great many doors, doors that need to be unlocked; doors that lead into a home where children and parents live with each other and enjoy the experience.

Chapter
5

Label
Them
Perfect

Picture yourself as a missionary sitting in a testimony meeting at a zone conference with some thirty elders and sisters. An elder stands to speak. All eyes are fixed upon him. The mission president and his wife are looking up at him from their seats. He starts to speak. His voice breaks with emotion as he looks into the eyes of the mission president and says: "President, you're a great man, and I love you. But I want to tell you something. You're not as great a man as my father. My father is the best man I've ever known."

The elder pauses. His emotions make it difficult for him to continue, because he has just made a statement that came right from the bottom of his heart.

As a mission president, whenever I heard an elder refer to his father in such a way I knew that there wasn't going to be any difficulty working with that elder. I knew that when a missionary thought of his father in that way he was in a state of mind that would make him a winner.

Now let's just have a look at this elder's father, this father whom we have just been told is a great man. You might say, "I'll bet he's a stake president." Well, he isn't. You might say, "He must be a bishop." But he isn't. You might say, "I'll bet he's a great speaker and teacher in the Church." He isn't. If we could see this father, we might even wonder why the elder said what he did. He might not look that impressive at all. He might be a most ordinary-looking man. He might not be anything great in the business world. He might have a job which seems quite unimportant. Now, this doesn't mean for sure he isn't a stake president — he might be, of course. It doesn't mean for sure he isn't a bishop. It doesn't mean he isn't a dynamic man. But these are not the things the elder is talking about.

You see, the elder is away from home; he has forgotten some of the faults his father has, and all he can see are those glorious traits that make his father his father. And that's why this statement, spoken with all the sincerity of his soul, coming from the bottom of his heart, thrills the souls of all those who hear it. This statement uttered about a father (and the same thing holds true for a mother) by a son or daughter tells us much about that son or daughter. If you could make such a statement about your parents right now, it could change your whole life. That doesn't mean that your father and mother don't have some faults. That has nothing to do with the fact that you feel that your father is the greatest man you know, or your mother the greatest woman. All you're stating is that in your opinion what you are saying about your father is true. And all that really matters in your heart is your own opinion, because it is your opinion that shapes your attitude, and it is your attitude that determines almost everything you do and attain.

Many (well, not *too* many!) years ago I was helping decorate for the senior dance at my high school. Into the hall walked a rather attractive woman. I was sort of surprised to find out that she was the mother of one of my classmates. This family had just moved into our town and I had never met the parents.

The woman commented on the decorations, then she said to her son, "Let's dance for a minute." He started dancing with her, and she was really a special kind of dancer. They went round and round as the rest of us watched in awe.

As I looked on, I found myself thinking, "It must be something to have a mom that looks young like that, a mom who can dance like that, a mom who just fits in with the gang the way she does."

For just a few seconds the thought flashed into my mind that I wished she was my mother. I wondered in my heart: "What would I do if my mom walked in? She's not young like my friend's mother. My mother is a little heavy and she just combs her gray hair straight back and fixes it in a bob at the back. I don't think she knows much about dancing at all."

As I stood there thinking, it occurred to me that I might be a little ashamed to have my mom come by while I was with my friends decorating for a dance. I felt bad about having that feeling, but that's the way I felt. At home I was really glad she was my mom, but sometimes out in public . . . I don't know. During my teenage years I started not wanting to have her come around when I was with my classmates. It wasn't because I didn't love her, it was just that I had the feelings which I've just described.

Maybe you have that feeling about your mom or dad sometimes. Maybe they're not impressive-looking, or maybe they aren't very flashy in public. I don't know what point I have in saying this, except that I want you to know how I felt just in case you ever feel that way. Later I felt very proud of my mother, felt it was grand to have her as my mom. Sometimes in the insecurity and thoughtlessness of our youthful years we overlook the true greatness of our parents because we put all the emphasis on physical appearances. When I grew up I learned to show my mom how proud I was of her. I hope you grow up much sooner than I did.

I recall coming home from my mission. There on the railroad platform was the girl I was going to marry, and near her was my mother. My girlfriend happened to be standing in a position where I got to her first. But I passed right by her and took my mother into my arms. If it hadn't been for my mother I'd never have been coming home from my mission, for she had taught me what I needed to know in order to be a missionary. It was she who had said she'd take care of the chicken farm while I was gone. She gathered eggs in the winter, summer, fall and spring, in snowstorms, rainstorms, and hot summer; because my father was sick, and my mother knew that the only way I could stay on my mission was for her to support me financially.

So I made certain that my mother was the first to receive my greeting as I arrived home. Later, of course, there was time for the girlfriend.

My point in saying this is that in high school I went from feeling a sort of shame to the point where I wanted the whole world to know who my mother was. Perhaps this will never be a problem for you; if it is, however, then the quicker you can make the transition the better. But for now, if you can't yet feel this way in public, at least let your parents know in private how much you love them and how much you appreciate them.

Sometimes you might see someone's dad and think, "Gee, if we had a dad like him in our house, things would really go well." Or: "Wouldn't it be nice if we had a mom like her? She's always so pleasant, so pretty, and so nice." If and when such thoughts come to you, remember that you can help to make your parents that way. Of course, you can't do it by preaching to them or by being ornery. But you can do it by treating them as if they were the kind of dad and mom you desire. Parents will respond to that. It's often been said that if you treat a person as if he is already what you recognize he could be, you help him to become that way. Parents are no exception to that rule. They respond when they see their children respect them and appreciate them. There's nothing so motivating to parents as to get the feeling, through words or deeds, that their children think they're pretty good parents.

The reverse kind of treatment from a son or daughter can be devastating to a parent. I once knew a young man who was in much trouble with the law. He and I had formed a friendship as I counseled him and tried to help him. He wanted his mother to come and meet me. He brought her over to my home and we talked for a long time. He played the piano for us. He was very talented, but he couldn't seem to follow the rules of society enough to stay out of jail.

After a long visit, and as he and his mother were about to leave, he said, "Brother Durrant, I just want you to know how I feel about my mom."

I was certain he was going to pay her a tribute, and I was taken aback as he continued: "I think she's the cause of most of my problems. I've always been ashamed of her.

She has never understood me. She has always done things that made me go wrong. She always let me do whatever I wanted. I was able to get my own way with her. I wouldn't be what I'm like today if it hadn't been for her. She knows my problems are largely her fault.''

I was shocked at what I was hearing, but he went on and on like that until I just wanted to hit him, though I don't think that's what he really needed. Finally he said he was going out to the car to get something. I told him: "Let me talk to your mother alone. Wait till I come out before you come back."

When he had left, I turned to his mother. "Ma'am," I said, "he doesn't know what he's talking about. I just want you to know that every mother makes some mistakes, but please don't let what he said wound your heart, because he doesn't know what he's saying. I can tell just from the time you've been here tonight that you're a great mother." I felt the Spirit then, and I think I was able to comfort her. I was so glad, because I've never seen a mother any more wounded by a son than she was at that time. I've never desired to comfort anybody so much in my life.

Whenever I hear a son or a daughter say degrading things to their parents it almost makes my heart bleed. Don't treat your parents that way. Treat them with respect wherever you are, in public or in private; just treat them as if they were a king and a queen. Treat your father like the provider he is, the breadwinner who has gone out to work each day over the years to feed and clothe his family. Treat your mother like the person who gave you birth, the magnificent person who has tried to raise you right.

It's true that in some cases parents might have been so permissive with a child that that is one of the things that has caused the problems of the son or daughter. But they did it because they loved that child, and they didn't know any better at the time, or they didn't feel strong enough to do better. I guess I'm preaching now, and people don't like to be preached at, but I have to say this: Don't ever do anything to break your mother's heart as that young fellow did. Don't do that to any degree. If you do and I ever find out about it, I'll come out of the covers of this book and I'll find you somewhere and (if you're not too big) I'll take you down and beat on you!

The best of all motivations by which to help your parents is to let them know in word and in deed that you think they are good parents. The words I spoke to that emotionally wounded mother gave her some comfort, but it was her son who had the power to make her the happiest of all women. He could have done that just by saying words such as: "Mom, I've been a real problem to you and to everyone, but it hasn't been your fault. You are the greatest mom in all the world." And if he could have said that and meant it, he would never again have seen the inside of a jail cell.

Your words of praise and your feelings of pride regarding your parents are part of the iron rod for you. If you cling to such things long enough and strong enough they will lead you to the joy of a happy home.

Chapter
6

Stress
Their
Strengths

In our relationships with friends we tend to overlook their faults and try to appreciate them for the good points they have. But sometimes at home it's different. Sometimes we act there as though we have a special license that allows us to criticize and be negative about other family members. There's something about the safety and security of home which seems to make us feel that we don't have to worry about the feelings of people there. So we say things at home that we wouldn't say to anyone outside the family.

To make it worse, it seems that too often we notice only the things that are wrong about family members. Now, in this book we're not talking about husband and wife relationships, though that's a very important area, for nothing in the world can destroy such a relationship faster than looking for the other person's faults rather than his or her virtues. Husbands and wives must learn this or their marriages cannot endure. But as teenagers we must learn this same lesson as regards our relationship with our parents. We must try to treat our parents as we would our friends. Where we see weaknesses we should overlook them; where we see strengths we should praise them. We should let our minds dwell upon strengths and not upon the weaknesses.

A young man I knew told me his father was gone from home too much. He said his father had a particular talent for helping other parents, so he spent his time on lecture tours that took him away from home. For the young man, this was a great source of ill feeling toward his father. Sometimes his father would come home and try in some great venture to make up for all the time he had been gone. "My dad would rent horses and we'd go up in the mountains and do all sorts of wonderful things," the young man told me. "But all the time we were there I couldn't get it off my mind that my father was trying to buy my love."

I told this story to my own children and they got quite disgusted with the attitude of the young man. They said, "Gee, Dad, we'd love you to take us on outings like those." One of my kids said, "That fellow just didn't have any appreciation." Well, that was easy for my children to say, because they weren't involved. When you're personally involved it becomes very difficult to see something clearly.

My heart is pained every time I read the experiences recorded in the book of First Nephi. The great man Lehi had had a vision. He knew that the whole future of the world depended upon the events he had seen in that vision. Have you ever stopped to think what would have happened if Lehi had decided just to stay home and not had the courage to go out and do what the Lord had told him to do? (Of course, the Lord would have raised up another prophet to do that particular work, but just suppose with me for a moment.) We would have no witness for Christ in America, no Book of Mormon, the keystone of our religion. It all came about because a great man named Lehi had the courage to follow the vision which the Lord had given him.

But it wasn't easy for his family. Sariah must have been a magnificent woman to have believed in the vision of her husband. She undoubtedly prayed and received a spiritual witness that what he was doing was right. She packed up her things and left a pleasant home to go out into the wilderness.

The entire family had to go. They were all treated in the same way. But Lehi's sons did not all respond in the same way. Why didn't they? They were all in the same situation. But we should never make the mistake of thinking that all the children in a particular family grow up under the same set of circumstances. Some are the oldest children, some are the middle children, some are the youngest children. Parents are younger when they're raising the oldest children, and older when they're raising the youngest children. Sometimes parents have more means when they're raising the younger children than they had when they were raising the older children. They learned many things as they raised the older children which will help or hinder them in raising the younger children. So we can't say that Nephi and Sam and Laman and Lemuel were raised in exactly the same environment. But they did have the same father and mother and much the same set of circumstances.

Nephi seemed to have the ability to understand what his father was trying to do. He had a vision much like Lehi's vision. He told his brother Sam of the vision and Sam believed him. But Laman and Lemuel refused to believe. When asked if they had inquired of the Lord about what their father had said, they replied, "No, for the Lord maketh no such thing known unto us." Thus they had a different way of looking at their parents than did Nephi and Sam. They saw only the bad. Nephi and Sam looked for and found the good. And that contrasting perspective made all the difference.

My son went through his teenage years in the mission field while I was mission president. At one point in time he was a little doubtful as to whether or not he would serve a mission. I didn't know what to do. I couldn't twist his arm and say that he had to promise me that he would. But I did remember that he was only seventeen. Sometimes people who are seventeen are not like they're going to be when they're nineteen. I prayed about it a good deal and talked to him as much as I could without seeming to preach to him. I had a fretful heart as I considered that he might not go.

I knew my son intended to go to BYU, however, and I hoped that when he got there he would get a religion teacher who would teach him the gospel in a way that would motivate him to want to go on a mission. Lo and behold, just as he enrolled at BYU, that school's officials called me and asked me if I'd come there as a religion teacher. Yes, you've guessed it! On the first day of class I looked down, and there, sitting on the front row grinning up at me, was my own son.

For two semesters, two hours a week I had the privilege of talking to him about the glorious truths in the Book of Mormon. Oh, there were others there, but I was talking to my son. We developed a choice relationship as we talked about these good things.

One day after class he came to me and said: "Dad, I have a question for you. I didn't want to ask you in front of the class because I know you won't know the answer, and I didn't want to embarrass you."

"What's your question?" I asked.

He responded, "How did Lehi feel when one President of the Church made the statement 'No other success can compensate for failure in the home'?"

That question would require some thought, so I replied, "I would like some time to think about your question before I respond."

The next day, after much prayer and consideration, I was ready, and I responded in class. I told the other class members of the question that had been asked me by my son. I went on to point out that Lehi was under great pressure as he went out into the wilderness and took his family with him. I told them that Laman and Lemuel did not understand what their father was trying to do.

I reasoned that perhaps Lehi had had his faults as he tried to teach his sons. Perhaps he was a little overbearing, or at least more so than some of those boys wanted him to be. And maybe they detected that he wasn't perfect. I don't intend to judge Lehi, but I suspect that he, like many of us, did not know how to relate perfectly to each of his children. I'm sure he wanted to, though. He must have had many heartaches as he tried to raise his family properly and at the same time do the thing that was required of him by the Lord to help mankind. I'm sure the mother, Sariah, had her sad times too. She must have tried with all her love, wisdom and patience to get the older boys to understand. But they simply wouldn't understand. They could only see the bad. They constantly wanted to turn back.

Now, there's nothing more difficult for parents than for them to try to accomplish something they know is right and to have their children constantly saying: "Let's go back. Let's not try to do it. It's too big for us. We can't do it. You're dumb for trying." Parents are not supermen. They can't constantly feel positive in attitude, cheerful, and strong when their children are negative, constantly complaining and wanting to go back. Parents can't feel good about themselves and happy about life if they feel that their children think they are not good parents.

On the other hand, Nephi seemed to understand his father and mother. He wanted with all his heart to see them succeed, he wanted to help them realize their dreams. He wanted to be part of that dream. As I taught the class that day, I read aloud to the students the words which Nephi spoke as he described his parents. And as I read I felt the Spirit as powerfully as I've ever felt it. I said to the class members: "If you desire to know what kind of father Lehi was, all you have to do is read the first verse in the Book of Mormon. Nephi there says of his parents, 'I, Nephi, having been born of goodly parents.' "

Now, these "goodly" parents were the same parents that raised Laman and Lemuel. Nephi saw them as goodly. I'm sure Laman and Lemuel saw them as just the opposite. You have to decide whether you want to see your parents through the eyes of a Nephi or through the eyes of a Laman and Lemuel. And the way you view your parents makes all the difference to them and to you.

Maybe your parents don't have any major faults. Maybe you see them as being almost perfect. There are parents who are absolutely and exceptionally wonderful. Then there are some that have a few faults. And there are some that have quite a few faults. And there are a few that seem to have very little at all to recommend them. Yet, in their private moments, almost all parents sincerely believe in good things for their children. If you can recognize and focus on the good things in your parents, then you will come to be able to say, as Nephi said, "I have been born of goodly parents."

If you can say that, your family, your friends and all who come in contact with you will be blessed by the experience. Most of all, gradually your parents will quietly begin to do those good things you would like them to do and you know they are capable of doing.

Try it. It won't happen all at once, but slowly you'll see the change. Just as the sun warms the earth, by your attitude and actions you will warm them. At the same time you'll be warming yourself. It won't be all that long before you'll find that your parents are "goodly."

Chapter
7

Talk
with
Them

My son was on the high school basketball team. At one point the coach advised the team members that he didn't think they were all doing as much as they should to be ready for the forthcoming tournament. He asked them all to make some special sacrifice with that in mind.

My son and some of the others decided that their sacrifice would be to get up early each morning and go over to school and practice basketball before school started. One morning while he was in the midst of this program I got up as early as he did so as to cook him breakfast. (His mother had had a broken sleep, and since it was now very early she remained in bed.)

We happened to have some bacon in the fridge. I cooked a lot more of it than I would have been able to had his mother been up. I fried him a few eggs. I made him some toast. I made him a drink by mixing some ice, some milk, some chocolate and a little ice cream. It was kind of a "good morning" milk shake. I had my son sit down at the table, then I served it all to him as if he were a king.

As he ate we talked. The only time my children have ever really talked to me is when I've been with them. He was most gracious as we talked, and we had a choice time together — just a father and son in that kitchen. When the food was all gone (and that wasn't long, the way he ate), it was time for him to go. He announced, "I've got to go quick, Pops" (that's what he calls me).

"Couldn't you just stay for a minute longer," I asked, "just long enough for you and me to kneel down and have a word of prayer?"

He could have said, "No, I've got to hurry," or he could have been ornery about it. But instead he quickly said: "Sure, Pops. There's always time for that."

He knelt down, and I knelt as close as I could to him. I acted as the voice for our prayer. I told Heavenly Father how grateful I was to have such a son. And in my prayers I poured out quite a few sentimentalities as I told the Lord how deeply I appreciated the way this young man was living and the things he was doing. I said so many things that the prayer was a rather long one. But he was patient and didn't seem to be fidgety, so I prayed on and on until I finally said amen.

After the prayer we both stood up. The Spirit of the Lord was present and my heart was filled with joy. I felt impressed to embrace my son and give him a kiss on the cheek. I don't do that often, but at that moment I just felt compelled to do it. Sensing what was happening, he didn't quickly take a karate stance as he could have done. Instead he embraced me and allowed me to kiss him on the cheek. As I did so I said, "Sure love ya." He looked at me with kind of a grin on his face and he said, "Sure love you, Pops." Then he turned and went towards the door.

Just as he was about to close the door, he looked back and grinned again. He almost laughed as he good-naturedly said, "Gee, Pops, I wonder how many other Provo High basketball players got a kiss from their dad before they went to school this morning?" I told him to get out of there or he would get something more than just a kiss — a kick in the pants. He laughed and hurried away. I watched him from the window until he was gone from sight. Oh, how I felt my love for him that morning!

Now it could be said that the story I have just related is a lesson for fathers and not for sons. After all, the father cooked the breakfast, said the prayer, and did the kissing. All the son did was eat. But my point is that the son did something vital to the experience. For, as you recall, he let his dad do these things. His reaction to my desire to show him how much I loved him was to go along with it. He didn't shrug it off and tell me to get away. Most parents would like to say, "I love you," but many are afraid it might not be well received.

What a help it is to your parents, at times when they try to show some affection towards you, if you just know how to receive it! By merely being willing to receive that affection you give them something special. (Of course, it's even better if you enthusiastically return it.) If parents have the feeling that you are willing to accept their humble offering of love and goodwill, it causes them to feel more courageous in expressing that love.

If your parents are not the sort who outwardly express love, then again the burden to help them rests squarely on your shoulders. Tell your parents how much you love them, and that will get them into the spirit of it. When somebody tells you they love you, it is much easier for you to say those words in return. All one man could ever say when someone said to him, "I love you," was "Me too."

But that's enough. When you say "I love you, Mom and Dad," something happens inside your heart and soul that causes an emotion to accompany the words, and your heart suddenly feels the message.

Once when my children were quite young we went to Lagoon, an amusement park near Salt Lake City. There they have what they call the "dodgem" cars. (You get into these electric cars and drive around and bump into other "dodgem" cars. You know the kind. They're great fun.) My family had been at Lagoon almost all day and we had finally decided to go home. As we assembled for the return journey, our oldest son was missing, even though he knew we were about to depart. We searched for him but couldn't find him. I finally gave up the search and went to the car to wait. As I waited I developed the kind of angry attitude that often comes to impatient fathers. I was most anxious to get home, as I had pressing matters to attend to there.

Finally my daughter came to me and said, "I found him, he's on the dodgem cars."

"Is he coming?" I asked.

"I told him to come," she said. "He got off when the dodgem cars stopped, but then he got back in line and got right back on again."

I could hardly believe it! He knew we wanted to go home, yet he had deliberately got back on those cars.

After we had waited some time my son showed up. All the way from Lagoon to Salt Lake City (which is some fifteen to twenty miles) I didn't even speak to him, or to anyone else. I'm much like many other fathers. I get angry and I quit talking. My son sensed my anger, so he didn't say anything either.

When we arrived home, my son went straight to his room while I sat down in the front room and began to work on some papers. I couldn't really concentrate on my work because by now I was over my anger and I was sorry I had become so upset over something so trifling. I felt as though I ought to go to his room and talk to him. About that time, however, his door opened and he came down the stairs. Halfway down he made an announcement: "Dad, I'm sorry." Then he said: "You want me to practice the piano. I'm going to practice the piano every day." He added: "I'm going to make it up to you, Dad, for not coming when you wanted me to come. I just want you to know that you're going to see a different son."

When he said those things I felt guilty for acting as I had. I told him I hoped that when he became old enough to drive a big car he would always obey the laws and principles about driving. We had a good talk about cars, and about other things too. I told him I was sorry for my behavior, and the two of us sat there and had a good talk.

Now, it was he who had opened the door that had been closed between us and had come back to me. To put things right, sometimes you just have to do that. Sometimes, like the prodigal son, you just have to come to yourself and come back. And this is so even if you feel that someone else was as much to blame as you or even more so.

I used to swing my children around by holding their arms and spinning around on the front lawn so that they would fly out parallel to the ground. It's great fun. Children love it. (It's getting harder for me to do. The older I get, the dizzier I get when I spin around.) I recall that once when I was doing this one of my little sons came running up and said, "It's my turn." At the same time my little girl who was nearby said it was her turn. I really felt it was my daughter's turn, so I said to the boy, "You wait, and I'll swing her first." While I was swinging her, he ran to the house in a rage. He lay down on his bed and continued his tantrum. He kicked his feet and looked up at the ceiling.

Time went by and he calmed down. He started to think. He had a decision to make. He could either stay there kicking like that and causing all kinds of trouble in his room, or he could just simply get off his bed and come back. I was still outside swinging kids around. After some time he decided to come back to the front lawn. He came running up to me and said, "It's my turn." And it was his turn. And I spun him around and he had fun.

Now, my son could have continued to stay in his room while I was still out there spinning people around. He could have lost out on that situation if he had wanted to. But he decided, as the prodigal son did, to come back. And when he came back I was ready with open arms to grab him and spin him around.

It's about as simple as that. You have to make a basic decision, as the prodigal son did. Of him the Savior said, "He came to himself." You just have to come to yourself, swallow your pride a little, and come back to your parents. Tell them you're sorry, even if sometimes you may think the fault is theirs. Someone has said, "You may be wrong and I may be right, but if it separates us we're both wrong." Come back and break through the barrier. And when you do you will be amazed at how anxious your parents are to make things right.

Sometimes you need an honest, frank discussion with your parents. Just before he departed on a mission my oldest son started writing the lyrics for songs. He wrote messages that emanated from his heart. His roommate, who was a fine piano player, would set the words to music. The two of them hoped to publish these songs.

One day I came home from work rather tired and wanted to relax and read the newspaper. But my son wanted me to come to his apartment; he had some songs he wanted me to hear. As we arrived at his room he was totally excited. His roommate began to play the piano and sing. I sat there and listened but I couldn't understand all the words because the piano was rather loud. I didn't understand the point of the words I could hear. I listened as intently as I could, but I didn't feel any great surge of enthusiasm for the songs; so I just said, "They are all right." Then I excused myself and departed.

About twenty-five minutes later my son arrived at our house and told me he wanted to talk to me. I asked him what he wanted to talk about. He said, "I want to talk about you." I could tell he was upset.

"Listen," he said, "I spent many hours writing those songs." And then he added in a very emotional tone, "I really feel good about those songs and that is why I invited you, my father, over to hear them."

He pointed his finger at me as he added: "I want you to know something. If you don't like the words to my songs, I want you to tell me you don't like them. And if you do like them, tell me so. But please don't just sit there acting as if you don't care. Please don't ever treat me that way again. And Dad, I hope you don't ever treat anybody that way again."

When he was finished, I knew I had just been talked to. I could have gotten angry, but because of the spirit in which he did it I could only admire him for his courage. I looked into his eyes and said: "All I can say, my son, is, I'm sorry. And I want to promise you that I'll do all in my power never to treat you or anyone else that way again."

He had taught me a monumental lesson, a lesson I needed to learn. We should never treat people with indifference. Perhaps the worst kind of treatment you can give anybody is to act as if you don't care. I appreciated that frank talking-to from my son. He could have just gone around harboring a grudge and it could have been a sore spot for him for years. But because he was willing to come to me and have some honest communication, we were able to overcome this problem instead of having it overcome us.

One girl told me that, years before, she had worked in a motel that her father owned. She and her sister were assigned to clean rooms. Her sister didn't like that kind of work and felt that some of the rooms she was assigned were bigger and harder to clean than the ones assigned to her sister. So upon the complaining sister's request, the two girls switched assignments.

According to the girl I was listening to, she really did a good job on her rooms. After the task was finished the father came and inspected the rooms, not knowing anything about the switch. He came to the girl who was telling me the story and said: "You can't ever do anything right. I've been in all the rooms. Your sister did a perfect job, but you didn't clean properly and you left things lying all around." He went on, "As far as I'm concerned you don't even have to help if you can't do it right."

The girl tried to explain, but he angrily interrupted her. "I don't want any excuses. I get so sick and tired of your excuses. You just can't seem to do anything right." Again the girl tried to explain, but he wouldn't listen and he stormed out.

Now, I wondered why her father would say things like that if she had never given him cause to think that way in the past. But in any event, she was sure his response was totally unfair at that point.

She told me that she had never again spoken to her father about that episode, but that it had always been a most painful memory to her. From that day on, that unresolved episode had made it impossible for her to have the kind of relationship with her father that she otherwise could have had. I don't know if he would have listened after he had cooled down, but what a blessing it would have been to him if she could have let him know what the truth of the matter was!

And what if she had approached him later and he still didn't understand or wouldn't accept her reasoning? Well, then she should take the position of the great man in the Book of Mormon named Pahoran.

The famous General Moroni wrote a letter to Pahoran, the chief judge and governor, and in one sense, unjustly criticized him and the other government leaders for things he thought were their fault. Moroni had no way of knowing the desperate problems that were facing Pahoran and the other leaders. He could only see the effects of their failing to support the fighting men; and his letter criticized them in a most severe way. Pahoran's only response to the penetrating rebuke was: "You have censured me, but it mattereth not; I am not angry, but do rejoice in the greatness of your heart." (Alma 61:9.) In other words, Pahoran was willing to forgive because of his own greatness. Sometimes we have to rise to greatness by being willing to forgive our parents when we feel they have acted unfairly toward us.

As a parent, I know that sometimes a difficulty comes up between two of my children and I don't really know all the circumstances. But I piece it together as best I can and as a result I frequently end up by criticizing one of the two children. And sometimes I'm wrong. Sometimes the situation turns out to have been entirely different from the way I sized it up. If something like that happens to you, if your parents get after you for some unjustified reason (unjustified in your mind, at least), then you ought to use the tactic that my son did and go and tell them about it. Before you go to do this most difficult task, pray about it, try to have the Spirit, and then do your best calmly to tell your parents how you feel.

On such an occasion if your parents won't accept your words, you've done all you can — at least, all you can at that time. Later you can try again. But in any event don't hold grudges against them. There's just no place for a grudge in a relationship between you and your parents. Grudge-holding is the very opposite of being forgiving, and it takes a lot of forgiving in any human relationship to be able to make it work. So remember to forgive your parents. That's just as good parent psychology as when you go to them and tell them you're sorry.

I hope you will forgive me for putting all the responsibilities on you. But what good would it do for me to advise you on what your parents should do? We can't change them in any direct way, but we *can* change you. And if we change you, maybe in time they will decide to change themselves.

When I think of seeking and obtaining forgiveness, I think of an experience my wife and I had some years ago when we were living in Brigham City, Utah. Our children had had a restless night. It had almost seemed as if they had conspired together, as if the oldest had said: "Now listen, fellows, here's how we'll do it. I'll cry from twelve to one, you wake up at one and cry from one to two, and then he'll wake up and cry from two to three. That way we kids can all get some rest, but we'll be able to keep Dad and Mom up all night."

So my wife had been up with the children most of the night. (The reason she was up and not me is that when my children cry at night I smile and I think, "That's one of my precious children." Then I nudge Marilyn and she gets up and I try to go back to sleep.) Neither of us got much rest that night, but she got less than I did.

The next morning I had to go to Salt Lake City early. I decided I'd quietly get out of bed and not even wake Marilyn up. I'd just prepare my own breakfast and do everything that needed to be done. (I'd say that's being rather a fine fellow, when I think about it.)

Starting to get dressed, I went to get a white shirt. There wasn't one ironed. As I asked myself, "Why hasn't she ironed my shirt?" I wasn't feeling quite as wonderful as I had felt ten minutes before. (Incidentally, every morning of my married life except that one she has had a shirt ready for me.)

A little disgruntled, I got a clean shirt and ironed it in the places where you have to iron a shirt if you're going to wear a jacket. At this point I was still feeling pretty good about myself. I then decided I would get myself some breakfast.

I set my mind upon some nice toast with honey. (I don't want to boast, but I make really good toast on our toaster.) But when I went to get out the bread — no bread! I looked in other possible places with the same result. It's difficult for even a talented person to make toast without bread, so by now I was upset. "Why isn't there any bread?" I thought to myself, "What does she do all day?" (Incidentally, there has been bread at home every morning except that one.)

As visions of toast and honey slipped away, I decided to make hotcakes. I began by following the recipe, but that was too slow. Because of the time factor, and because I decided I knew what things went into hotcakes, I discarded the recipe. Hurriedly throwing in my ingredients, I mixed them all together.

Finally the hotcakes were done and I sat there in a lonely kitchen and started to eat. The first mouthful was terrible and all the others more than matched it. With each bite I took I became more and more upset until I was almost beside myself with disgust, frustration, and self-pity.

Now, perhaps you've noticed that it's no good being upset if you're all alone. It's just a waste of energy. So, if you're going to be upset, you've got to be able to show somebody you're upset. I knew that the best way to show people that I'm upset is just to be quiet, not say anything. Then when they say, "What's wrong with you?" I can say, "Nothing's wrong! Why do you think anything's wrong?" Pretty soon then I'm getting even more mileage out of my "upset" condition.

But that method doesn't work if you're alone, because there's nobody there to see that you're being quiet and not speaking. So, realizing on this occasion that the silent treatment wouldn't work, I decided to use "Plan B." This plan is just the opposite of silence; it consists of "banging around." So I banged around.

You can really bang around in great style in the morning when others are asleep. I banged around and banged around until I knew I'd awakened Marilyn, then I went into the bedroom for the final part of my act. There was a sliding door on the closet which contained my suit coat, and I knew that if I slid it with great vigor it would hit against the other side and make the last big bang. In case any doubt remained, that would definitely let Marilyn know that I was upset. So I vigorously slid the door across and it banged on the other side. Out of the corner of my eye I saw that Marilyn jumped at the noise. Now I knew she was awake.

I then made a cold and calculated decision that I would really let her know how upset I was. I would just put on my coat and leave without saying good-bye. And that's what I did. And that's how I left the house that morning, I who was supposed to be a "priesthood man," a man who everybody at church thought was a fine fellow and all that sort of thing.

At the time I was a branch president and had an office in the nearby chapel. I now went down to that office to get some papers to take to Salt Lake City to my meeting. As I picked up the papers it occurred to me that I should pray, because that's what I did every morning in the office. So I knelt down to pray. As I was praying there was only one thing that I could think about, and that was to ask Heavenly Father to bless my wife Marilyn that she would have a happy day. I asked the Lord for that blessing for her, and after that request I couldn't think of anything else to say. As I knelt there speechless, Heavenly Father spoke to me. At least, he put an idea into my mind. He suggested: "Why don't you go home and bless her? You're closer to her than I am."

As I arose from my knees, I knew that in order to bless her I had to do one of the hardest things in the world. I had to give the most difficult speech there is to give. Short as it is, it's terribly hard to deliver. I rehearsed it in my mind and I prayed for the courage to be able to say the words. I went home, and for some reason Marilyn was up and around. (Apparently something had awakened her earlier.) As I approached her I looked into her eyes and I could see the hurt that was there. I took a deep breath and gave the speech. I said, "Marilyn, I'm sorry." Then came the speech that regularly follows the words "I'm sorry," spoken between family members, and it goes, "And I love you." And there's something that follows those words, when spoken to one's wife or husband, and it's not a speech at all. I hurried out of the house again. This time I was a real priesthood man and I was ready to do the Lord's work. And, by the way, Marilyn told me that she did have a happy day.

To live with your parents and like them, one of the speeches you have to learn to give to them is the message, "I'm sorry." Whenever you feel that way, be sure to tell them so. And when you do they usually will respond with the words, "I'm sorry, too." When that's done, the fence is mended. A prodigal has come back. (And I'm not saying who the prodigal is, because sometimes it's your parents.) Words of sincerity such as "I'm sorry," "I love you," "Will you forgive me?" "I'll try to do better," "I want to be like you, Mom" are the kind of words that make the relationship between you and your parents a thing of beauty forever.

Learn to talk to your folks about things that interest them. Learn something about what your father does where he works. I often ask young people what their father does at work, and I'm amazed at how many of them say, "I really don't know." You ought to know what your father does for the living he provides for the family. You ought to be able to talk to him about it. You ought to be able to tell him that you admire the things he does.

Another piece of parent psychology as you talk to them is to strive to motivate your father and mother to have hobbies and special interests. My oldest son said to me one day, "Dad, you're too lazy to write a book." He added: "I know of a medical doctor who has written a book and he's a lot busier than you. But you'll never write a book. You're too lazy."

It wasn't two weeks after that until I had started on my first book. When I had completed the manuscript, I threw it down in front of him and said, "There you go!" I added, "Too lazy, huh?!"

He responded: "I knew you could do it, Dad. But I knew I had to goad you or you'd never get at it."

Take an interest in what your dad's doing. If he's a

mechanic, learn something about mechanics and talk to him about it. Even if you want to be an artist and not a mechanic, that's no reason to turn your back on everything he's doing. I haven't got much patience for any young person who feels that his father's work is too menial or trivial. Maybe you are an artist or are going to major in English or music. That's good and right, if it's right for you, but learn what your dad is doing in his trade or his profession and learn to talk to him about it. Ask him once in a while how things went at work that day.

I have one son who at one period used to call me down to his room every evening. "Pops, come on down to my room," he'd call out. I'd call back, "I'm too tired." And he'd say, "Pops, if you knew how much it meant to me, you'd come down."

Now, what other choice did I have when my son treated me like that? He wanted me to go down, so I did. I'd sit down and he'd say: "How did it go at work today, Pops? What happened?"

We'd look at each other and exchange grins, and sometimes I'd ask, "What do you want to know for?" He'd reply: "Because I'm interested in you, Pops. I'm interested in your progress and how you're doing." So I'd start talking, telling him things that had gone on at work that day. Then I'd ask, "How did it go with you?" We'd more or less give each other a report, and then he'd say: "Okay, Pops, you can go. I just want to keep track of what you're doing."

Those were such special times for me. They were as a priceless gift from my son.

Another tip on talking to your parents is not to question their memory too much about their tougher childhood experiences. When your dad tells you that as a child he walked to school six miles through the snow every day with no shoes, act somewhat as if you believe him. Let him be responsible if it's not all quite true. Tell him something like, "Boy, they made kids tough in those days!" (Not sarcastically, of course.) If he's told you the same story before, don't say, "You've said that a thousand times, Dad." After all, there's a good chance he's only told it 990 times.

Do you feel that your parents ask dumb questions? Don't tell them their questions are dumb. That kind of response really turns parents off. Through their dumb questions, they're just trying to find out some things. They're not prying. When your dad says, "What did you have at school for lunch?" don't say, "That's a dumb question." When he asks you how you did in the basketball game, don't tell him that's a dumb question. When he says to you, his daughter, "Did anybody compliment you on your hairdo?" don't tell him that's a dumb question. Just answer the questions as though they were really intelligent questions. Just remember that there's no such thing as a dumb question when it's asked by somebody who is trying to show an interest in you.

In other words, "talk to your parents." If you talk to them they'll respond, and as you and your parents communicate, you'll come to love them dearly.

Chapter
8

Do Things for Them

My father raised chickens and we sold the eggs. That's how we made a living. Because cracked eggs didn't sell, my mother would use them in her cooking.

One day she said in dismay, "Oh, I wish I could make a cake; but there aren't any cracked eggs, so I guess I can't." My older brother thought for just a moment, picked up two whole eggs, banged them lightly together, and handed her the cracked eggs. "There, Mother," he said, "I've solved your problem. Go ahead now and make the cake."

Mother was speechless for a second or two, but then she smiled; and soon there was a cake. When you do things for your parents, it seems that the result is always a cake of one type or another.

I recall finding out how much my father liked ice cream. This was back in the "olden days" when we didn't have refrigerators and there was no way to keep ice cream at home. Sometimes on a summer evening I would jump on my bike and ride down the old Alpine Road as fast as I could go to buy a pack of vanilla ice cream. In those days it didn't come already packaged. At the drugstore they would dip it out of a large container and put it in a small cardboard package. (They'd really heap it all up; the top wouldn't even close.) Then they'd put the package in a sack. I'd grab the sack fast, race home on my bike, and hurry in the house.

My father would be sitting over in the corner of the room in his old rocking chair (that's where he always used to sit) and he'd grin when he saw the package. I'd dish him out a heaping dish of ice cream and take it over to him. Then I'd get myself a dish and sit there with him. He wouldn't say much to me nor I to him, but we'd sit there and eat ice cream together. It was wonderful to be with my father. We didn't have very many conversations, but getting that ice cream was good parent psychology. My father loved it when he was eating ice cream, and that was just about my favorite indoor sport too. With every little taste bud soothed into a state of blissful rapport we just seemed to communicate, even though we didn't use a lot of words.

By getting my dad the ice cream I was doing something for him. As a parent I am highly in favor of my children doing things for me. It recalls the scriptural adage that it is more blessed to give than to receive. I like my children to enjoy the blessings which come from giving. In order to help them have the opportunity of giving, Christmas is the time that I'm willing to increase their allowance by any amount they desire, just as long as the money is used for presents for their mother and me. I'm willing to be on the side of the lesser blessings (the receiver) so that my children can be the givers. I guess I'm just a naturally unselfish fellow.

It is not easy to truly love somebody you're not serving.

The reason why parents generally love their children is that they do so much for them — particularly when the children are small. There is no love to match the love a mother has for an infant. That's because the mother is constantly doing things for the infant.

I went to Primary faithfully all during my childhood. I hardly ever missed, and I have several books to attest to my faithful attendance. Whenever they would give me a treat in Primary, I would want to take it home to my mother and share it with her. I remember one early spring day when it was very warm outside. The treat that day was an ice cream bar. I stuffed it in my pocket and took off for home. When I arrived, the ice cream bar had become something closer to a milk shake. Mother didn't share it with me, but just the fact that I'd brought it home seemed to please her. Doing that for her made me love her all the more. I was especially happy when she didn't spank me for getting my trousers' pocket rather sticky and gooey.

One father, while looking in the mirror and combing his hair, asked his daughter, "How many truly great men do you think there are in the world, honey?" And she replied: "I don't know, Dad. But because of you, there's one more than there otherwise would have been." Wasn't it nice of her to say that?

When he asked, "How many great men do you think there are in the world?" his daughter could have replied in fun, "I don't know, but there's one less than you think." Either way she would have made her father a winner. It's a blessing when children compliment you, their parents, but it's also a blessing when they tease them and have fun with them. You have fun with everybody you love. I don't mean sarcastic teasing, but the kind of fun and games you have with people you really like and in whose company you feel relaxed.

I know my son is forever asking his mother, "How's my best girl friend?" He does it with great emphasis. He says, "You must be the most beautiful woman in all this town." She kind of shrugs it off, but after he's said that to her a few times he surely gets a lot of special favors around the house.

While I was growing up, I don't recall that my family ever had family prayer. Just before I was to go on my mission, I was alone with my father and we had a chance to talk. He expressed to me in his own way that he loved me. Then the family all started to gather at our house prior to going over to the church for my farewell. Some of them didn't go to church regularly, but they were nevertheless a fine family.

With the family all there, as a young man just about to go on a mission I said, "I believe it's Dad's desire that all of us kneel down and have a prayer." I continued, "Dad, if you'd like I'll offer the prayer." It took a lot of courage for me to do that, but I did it because my father was sick at the time and he really didn't think I'd get home from my mission before he died. With that thought in mind, in one way he really didn't want me to go, I believe, though for my sake he was glad I was going. Anyway, he was worried.

We knelt down and I began, "Heavenly Father, please bless my father." As I said that I had a kind of revelation, and I added, "for I know that his health will be sufficient that when I return he will still be here. I love him very much." I said some other things about the family, and when I said amen I got the feeling that our family was closer and more united than they had ever been before. As my father looked at me I could see how pleased he was with the prayer and how much faith he put in it; how glad he was that he'd seen his family take the opportunity of kneeling together in prayer.

I believe we children can have a profound influence in helping our parents have family prayer and family home evening and in helping them do all the things that would make the home better. Children can exert that kind of influence when they're young and also when they're older.

I know a fine family who are desirous of doing what they should. For some time, though, they never seemed able to have daily scripture reading as a family, as Church members are expected to (even though the father was very anxious to do it). He tried repeatedly to get the family members up and reading in the morning. But it's hard to get teenagers up. He struggled with the problem for some time, but there was always a somewhat negative atmosphere as he tried to force the issue. He expressed to me that he had a feeling of failure as regards this great principle of family scripture reading.

Later he told me how one night in a family home evening, when he started to bring this subject up, his daughter, a beautiful senior in high school, said: "Dad, I've been thinking about this and I want you to know that from now on you can count on this family. We're going to read the scriptures daily, and I'm going to see to it that everybody gets up and is ready to do it."

As my friend told me this, tears came to his eyes. "I've never had such a thrilling spiritual experience in my life," he said, "as to have my daughter say that." He continued: "Every day since then she has gotten everybody up, and she has done it in a very pleasant way. She gets all the books ready and makes it possible for us to have daily scripture reading. I had wanted to do that all along and I just couldn't get it going. But my daughter has helped me do it."

As he related this story to me my eyes were moist with

tears. What a joy it is when the young people of the family take it upon themselves to help the parents accomplish righteous goals! Maybe your folks aren't religious, or don't go to church. If so, preaching to them may not be the answer. You have to be sensitive and wait for the right moment. Now and again some right moments will come up, and then you can inject things into family life that will make it better. Your parents need your help. And when they see that you're helping them they feel an increasingly greater love for you, and suddenly your feelings toward them are warmer than ever before.

Sometimes in walking home from sacrament meeting I ask some of my little children what the speaker talked about. They're not always sure. Sometimes they say things to me like, "Daddy, give me a hint." But sometimes they know, because somebody has told a story. Now, of course, our talks in church shouldn't normally consist of just stories. But it is a good thing when once in a while a speaker tells a story that the children can relate to.

I notice that in our meetinghouses now there are little drinking fountains as well as bigger ones. I wish that everybody who is about to give a talk in church would look at those drinking fountains before he speaks, in that way being reminded to say something to the little children as well as to the older people.

At any rate, one young man told the following story in our sacrament meeting:

"One morning I arose from my bed and came into the kitchen where some of the other family members were. They asked me, 'Did you leave the water running outside last night?'" Whoever had done so had left the hose close to the basement window, and the water had flooded the basement.

"I said I hadn't left it running, but somebody else said

he knew I had. Father said, 'I think it was you; you were out there last.' There were some sharp exchanges of words, and the family had kind of an argument. There was a negative feeling in the home. I felt that I'd like to tell everybody off, and even that I'd like to punch a few of them.

"Then Dad looked at the clock and said, 'Well, I've got to go to work. It's time we had family prayer.' I felt like saying: 'What do you mean, family prayer? We don't have the right to have family prayer, the way we act and shout at each other. Besides that, everybody has accused me falsely for something I didn't do.' But I didn't know what else to do, so I knelt down. Then to top it all off my father looked at me and said, 'It's your turn.' He said it rather sharply. I looked at him and he looked back at me. He finally out-looked me, so I closed my eyes and said, 'Heavenly Father.' And then I didn't know what else to say.

"After a while, I said: 'We haven't got any right to pray. We've got a lot of contention and dissension in our home.' My spirit changed a bit when I said that. I continued to pray by saying: 'Heavenly Father, we don't want to act in this way. Help us that we can talk to one another in a normal way and love one another and not accuse one another. For everything we've done wrong we're sorry. Please help us to have love in our home.' Then I said amen.

"I stood up and my prayer was answered immediately. The whole spirit in our home was changed by that prayer. I looked at my dad and my dad looked back at me, and we embraced; and I kissed my mother. My brothers and sisters gave me a warm look. We just all felt like standing there and singing a chorus of 'There is beauty all around when there's love at home.'

"My brothers and sisters, I know that family prayer works, because it works for us."

When my family were on the way home after that meeting, I asked the children, "What did that fellow say in church tonight?"

"Oh, Dad," they responded, "he said that their family is just like ours. He said that they sometimes have trouble at home. He said they have family prayer and it really works. And we believe it works, too. We loved his talk."

The young man who gave that memorable talk, when asked by his father to pray, could have said, "I'm not going to pray." Instead he was willing, or at least felt impelled, to honor his father's request. He went ahead even though it was difficult to do so, and his prayer restored the family to what it should have been. Through his efforts they were all made to feel the joy of repentance.

This may not be too exceptional an experience in LDS homes. And who got the family back on the right track? One of the younger members — someone about your age, perhaps. You can't just leave it all to your parents. They're not a superior species. They're just like you. Frequently, then, the burden is right upon your shoulders and nobody else's. When you come through, what a blessing it is to the family!

Now, I know that some of you are not going to have a desire to lead the family in prayer or to make family home evenings better. But when you see the results of this kind of thing, then your desires might change a little. You know, we're all trying to find our place, trying to find happiness. But it's when we finally start to lose ourselves that we begin to find real happiness.

Jesus said, "He that loseth his life shall find it." When you do things for the family, for your father and mother, you're doing the kind of losing your life that will help you to find it. I'm talking about going on a picnic with your family instead of going out with the guys; going to a family reunion with them when you would rather have stayed home and listened to your music; doing things not because you want to but because you know your parents want you to. When you do these kinds of things, then something happens inside both you and them that makes the relationship much more beautiful.

Your parents may not be members of the Church. Maybe it's your father who is not a member, or your mother, or maybe both. Of course, with all your heart you want to bring them into the Church. Jeremiah said that Israel would be gathered "one of a city and two of a family." This perhaps means that if you have joined the Church there is an excellent chance your parents will too.

Sometimes, though, you just have to restrain yourself in preaching to your nonmember parents. Instead just go home and do things for them. Show them the fruits of the gospel in your life. Be willing to go out of your way to serve them. Start with little things perhaps — get them an ice cream cone, bring them something they like such as a cold drink from the fridge — then move gradually into acts which expend your time and energy and save theirs.

As you do these things for them and with them, talk to them and tell them how much the gospel means to you. Don't always act as if they have to join the Church. Wait for the opening. Leave a Book of Mormon around the house. But basically just *do things for them.* If they are clearly willing, ask a blessing on the food. In the blessing say something like: "Heavenly Father, bless my dad and mom and help them. They're such good people and I'm so proud to have them for my parents." You can say many effective things in prayers which can't readily be said at other times.

Another good place for saying important things is letters. When you write letters home, use words of love and encouragement. These are the kinds of things that are going to make your folks happy, and they could even cause them to desire to know more about the Lord and his church.

Be sure and laugh at your father's jokes. You don't have to laugh unless they are appropriate jokes, but if he tells a joke that really is funny, don't boo him and then go off in a corner and laugh. (That's what my children do.) Laugh right in front of him. Tell him, "Dad, that was a superb joke!" Most men would like to think they've got a little bit of the comedian in them. Some children say to their dad, "Fifty thousand comedians out of work, and you're trying to be funny." But even a "boo" at Dad's joke makes him feel good.

I made up a joke one evening when I was out with my children. As we walked along I said, "Hey, kids, I've got a joke." I continued, "If a man named Richard was to take a potato and carve it out so that it was shaped like a little boat, what would you have?"

After thinking for a while, they said, "We don't know, Dad."

"Well," I said, "you'd have a Dick Tater Ship."

They laughed and laughed. "Gee, Dad, you're really clever," they said. I felt good about that all night because my kids had thought I'd told a really good joke.

As well as being told they're clever, fathers need to be told they're handsome. Well, most of them do, though I'm an exception to that rule. I just have to check that one out in a mirror; nobody has to tell me. (I thought I'd just mention my good looks in case you might not notice.) Nevertheless, once in a while it makes me feel good to have my children say, "That's a nice-looking suit, Dad," or "I like your hair, you must have just got it cut." One of our children told my wife, "The mother of one of my friends said, 'Your mother sure is beautiful.' " When you hear a compliment about your parents, rush home and let them know. It will make their day.

When I was growing up I would come home every night, put all the chairs around the round table in our big kitchen, and sweep the floor. Having done that, I felt that I could sincerely leave my mother a note saying, "Mom, I love you." I don't think you should ever say anything insincere to anybody about how you feel about them. But when you do nice things for them, then it gets you feeling good about them. Then you want to say so, and you leave them a note or something to tell them how much you appreciate them.

I know one young man who gives his mother a present every year on *his* birthday. He tells her, "Mother, I feel that because you gave me this precious birth, I want to do some little thing for you." So he gives her a gift every year.

And what a joy it is for the parents when their children sit by them at church! After my son had blessed the sacrament one day, he made what looked like a beeline toward the back of the chapel. Suddenly he made a sharp left turn and sat down right by me. He put his big hand on my shoulder and whispered, "How's it going, Pops?" I whispered back, "It's really going well, Son." As I sat there by him I felt like a million-dollar man. I don't know why it is such a thrill for dads to sit next to their kids but it is, especially when they are old enough that they don't cry in church anymore (I mean the kids, of course).

When my children were little, I used to enjoy it more sitting on the stand in church. I would let my wife deal with them when they were noisy. As a leader I had a good excuse for sitting on the stand. It sure is a lot easier sitting on the stand when your kids are little than it is to sit in the audience with them. May the Lord bless all those glorious mothers who fight the battle in the congregation with the children while Dad sits up on the stand in some capacity or another. But you ought to know, now that you're older, how pleased it makes your parents feel to have you sit with them in church.

One of the greatest difficulties we have in our lives is trying to be pleasant rather than ornery. Once in a while I guess you just have to go ahead and be ornery. I know that during your teenage years, when you're growing and changing, you often get frustrated at school and in other places where things aren't going so well. During those trying times it's hard to be pleasant. But make the effort. Try to be pleasant, if you can.

One of my sons once told me, "Dad, if I acted at school the way I act around home sometimes, I'd never have a friend."

I was just opening my mouth to agree with him when he continued: "It's just that here at home I come in and I feel that I want to be ornery and so I'm ornery. At school I can't be ornery or I'd lose all my friends. I'm sorry, Dad. I'll try to be better."

Just having him say that made me feel happy. He was doing something he knew I would like. After that he was still pretty ornery but at least I knew he was trying, and I know how hard it is sometimes to be pleasant.

When you do feel pleasant, why not let it be known? You might even come out of your room and call out to everybody, "I'm pleasant, I'm pleasant." Then they can see that you are pleasant once in a while. Remember that even nearly perfect people can be unpleasant at times, but the fact that they're nearly perfect means that at least they don't *want* to be unpleasant.

These are some of the things you need to struggle with, some of the things you ought to do for your parents, if you want to have a happy home life. The real secret to being able to live with your parents and like them is to be able to live with yourself and like yourself. Now, those who know tell us that the best way to like yourself is to start reaching out and see how much good you can do for others. Trying to show the spotlight on somebody else causes a light to shine within you that makes you glow as if you were yourself a spotlight. And once that has happened you can be a light to your parents, a light that will make them and you members of the happiest of families.

Chapter

9

Take Their Advice

One of the most intelligent uses of parent psychology is to listen to your parents and do what they advise. I asked my children if they knew of any examples of children taking parents' advice, so that I could include those examples in this book. They said, "No, Dad, we can't remember any time we ever took your advice." I spanked them on the spot and told them to cry; and that time they took my advice.

When I was in the first grade, school lasted only a half a day for that particular grade. All the other grades went for the full school day. I walked to school with my older brother, and one day when we arrived at the building his friends met us and suggested that we all sluff school that day. At that stage of my development I didn't even know what *sluff* meant. They explained that it meant to go up in the creek bed and play instead of going to school. I didn't know how to read and write very well, but I did know a good idea when I heard it; so I quickly sustained that particular motion and we headed over to the creek bed.

It was a magnificent place to play. The stream was running, we threw into it the bottles that some of the town's men had thoughtfully emptied and left along the banks the night before. As the bottles bobbed up and down on the water, we would throw rocks at them and play as though we were throwing rocks at ships. After we tired of that we'd go and lift up pieces of metal from old wrecked cars nearby. As we did so the lizards would dash out from underneath and we'd chase the lizards and capture them and put them in bottles. Then we'd let them go. I don't think I'd be overrating it to say we had a magnificent experience there that morning.

Finally the others decided it must be almost time for me to go home, because I had to go home at noon, whereas they didn't go home from school until about three o'clock. We had no watches, so my brother and his friends fashioned a sundial; and after some degree of calculation they announced, "It's noon, you'd better head for home."

Taking their word on faith, I made my way toward home. I was approaching the house with a smile on my face when my mother, who was looking through the front window, saw me coming. She came out on the porch to meet me.

"Hi, Mom," I said.

Instead of greeting me as she usually did, she said, "How come you're home a half-hour early?"

"Well, it's after noon, isn't it?"

"No, it's eleven-thirty. How come you're home early?"

I stood there for a few seconds, not knowing what to say. As I looked around I noticed down in the southern sky, in the middle of all the blue, a little white cloud. I decided I'd better think fast, and that's exactly what I did.

"Well, Mom," I said, "see that cloud down there in the sky?"

"Yes," she said.

"The teacher saw it too," I explained. "She thought that might be a storm coming, and she said we'd all better leave school and get home before it started to storm."

From the way my mother looked at me I could tell immediately that she didn't believe me. So I told her the entire truth; I guess I sort of turned "state's evidence." After a severe talking-to (and a spanking that I almost got, but not quite), she asked me to promise never to sluff school again. As I promised her, I thought to myself: "I can't fool her. My mom knows everything. I'd better not ever try anything like that again." And for a long time I didn't.

I found out at that early age that my mom knew some things that were almost outside the scope of human reason. Now, I'll admit it wouldn't have taken a Sherlock Holmes to figure out my particular case of The Boy Who Came Home Early. But there have been other cases in which it was absolutely amazing how my mom seemed to know things that I ought to do and other things that I ought not to do. She could see the whole situation clearly when I couldn't see it at all.

I recall that once, when I was much older than I was the day I sluffed school, several of my friends said they had a trip planned to Las Vegas and asked if I could go with them. I think I was a senior in high school at the time. You know, that's about the age when you start thinking you can make your own decisions. I told Mom that I was going to Las Vegas with my buddies. She calmly asked me what we were going down for, how long we would be gone, and so on. I gave her what I thought were good answers. I was polite and kind and considerate.

She didn't say much more about it, and finally it came time for us to go. I had a little bag packed; and as I walked out toward the car my mother followed me out. "George," she said, "come back just a minute, will you?"

I said, "Sure, Mom," and stepped back into the house.

"George," she said, "don't go."

"Gee, Mom," I protested, "they're waiting for me. I promised to go. I want to go. It'll be a good little vacation for me, and I've got the money to go."

"George, don't go," she repeated.

"But why, Mom?" I asked.

"I don't know why," she replied, "but please don't go."

"Mom, I've got to go," I insisted.

Yet again she said, "Don't go."

Now a strange feeling began to come over me. "Mom, why?" I asked again.

This time she said, "I just know you shouldn't go."

The feeling had now become so overwhelming that I just walked out of the house and said to my friends, "I can't go."

They began to get upset. "Why not?" they asked.

I replied, "Because my mom says I shouldn't go."

Of course, they tried to persuade me, then finally to taunt me into going. "Ah, come on. What are you, some kind of a mama's boy?"

I simply said, "No, I'm not a mama's boy, but she said I shouldn't go and I'm not going."

They finally gave up on me and drove away in some degree of disgust.

Two days later I learned that my friends' car had turned over several times as they were travelling down the highway late at night and that all four of those fellows had been thrown out. Not one of them had been seriously injured; one was knocked unconscious for a time, but he was revived and he had no aftereffects. The police officer said it was a miracle someone hadn't been killed. I've always wondered what would have happened if there had been five fellows in that car. I wonder if five would have been as lucky as four. I guess I'll never know. But I do know that my mom knew I shouldn't go; and I know now, as I knew then, that she was right.

As a parent, while my family and I were living in Kentucky, I ran into a somewhat similar experience with my son. It was the custom of the high school kids, particularly the seniors, to go to Florida for the spring vacation. It was just the thing to do. My son was a junior that year, and all of his friends had decided to go. His mother and I had many talks about it, and he never quite seemed to understand why we didn't want him to go.

His mother was home more than I was and consequently had more talks with him than I did. After a couple of weeks he was a little upset about the whole thing. He insisted that he wanted to go; that his friends were going and he intended to go with them.

Finally the day came when he had to make the decision to either follow or not follow our advice. He went to school, and while there I guess he decided to make one last appeal. He phoned home and said: "Mom, I want to go. My friends are all going, and I'm coming home to get my bags."

Much the same as my mother had said to me years before, his mother said, "Don't go."

"But I *want* to go," he insisted.

Again she said, "Don't go."

Then to her surprise he responded in a pleasant voice, "All right, Mom, I won't." Later he told her: "I just turned to my friends and said, 'I'm not going.' They seemed to understand."

The next year that son was a senior, and that year he and my wife and I all felt good about his going on that traditional spring vacation. He went and he had a glorious experience, one that I think he will remember forever. But the year before that it just wasn't the time. His mother knew it just as I did, and finally he took her advice. It's such a blessing to have a mother who has that insight that makes all things turn out right if you follow her advice on the matters that are really important.

Fathers too can display great wisdom. I know of one young man who wanted to get advice from his Church leader, advice about his girl friend and his prospective marriage and a number of other personal matters. He particularly admired this leader, so he went to him and asked for advice.

The leader's advice was, "Go home and talk it over with your father." The young man became quite irritated at this. "My father wouldn't understand this," he said. "I don't talk to him about such things."

When he saw this leader some time later he told him what had happened. "I was most upset with your counsel at the time," he said, "but some days later I was hauling hay with my father. As we worked together I got to thinking about what you had said, and I decided to ask his advice as you had suggested."

He continued: "We sat down on a bale of hay and talked. I was amazed at my dad's response. I didn't think he understood about such things. But he told me about how he met Mom and about their courtship. Suddenly I found myself enthralled with what he was saying. I asked him more and more searching questions about things. The answers he gave me seemed to ring loud and clear and true to me. I took my dad's advice. It turned out to be exactly the right advice."

Yes, there is great wisdom available from our parents. They might appear to be "old fogies" at times, but they've been down a longer road and they've seen many things their children have not seen, and thus they have a greater perspective.

Mention of perspective makes me recall a film made for the seminaries. It shows a huge buck deer — a mighty stag — standing upon a high mountain viewing the panorama before him. Down on the highway he sees two young spike deer running and playing together. Instantaneously he can see in his mind's eye the scene of many years earlier when he had been frolicking on that same highway with another young deer. Around the corner had come a huge truck. He had been able to jump to safety just in time; his young friend hadn't been so fortunate and was hit by the truck and killed.

The stag now takes off, crashing through the timber as he runs down the mountain at great speed. He reaches the bottom, but as he approaches the two young deer two questions loom large in his mind: "What will I do? What will I say?"

So often those who are at a higher point, who have lived longer and have more experience and perspective, can see "afar off." You need to listen to them and follow their advice. I'm not saying that they are more intelligent than you or that you're not going to go a lot further in life than they have, but that doesn't mean they can't give you some very wise counsel at this point in your life.

You know, when our Heavenly Father planned to send his spirit children to earth in mortal bodies he had to have a continuing program for their guidance and development. He arranged for this through the family system. Their earthly parents were to take care of and train his children in the earlier years of mortality; then the children themselves could later take on parenthood and continue the program.

Now, it wouldn't have made much sense in this training program if the parents had been given only the same degree of knowledge and understanding as their children. So actually there's a special blessing given to parents that equips them for the task. The Lord endows parents with wisdom to impart to their sons and daughters. As the young people listen to that wisdom, it's amazing how many good leads they can get on good things.

Some of us are always willing to listen to our parents, while probably others are willing to listen on occasion. But if you really want to enjoy the experience of living with your parents, what a blessing it would be if you would actively seek their advice!

Even if your dad isn't active in the Church, it's probable that no Church leader could give you any better advice than he can. Of course, it helps if he is active because Church activity has a lot to do with a lot of important things, and we would all want him to be active for his own sake and the family's. But regardless of that, with his love and concern for you he may have just the right kind of input for you. The Lord knows that he's the head of the house and will honor him as such and give him insights that he will be able to communicate to you. Mothers too will often have an intuitive feeling that helps them give wise counsel to their children.

So seek your parents' advice. Listen to their advice. Take their advice. And when you do and it works out, tell them so. "Dad, your advice was most helpful. You told me what to do and I did it and it really worked." That's going to do a lot for Dad. It will make him think, "I guess I'm not such a poor father after all." There's no greater way to honor your parents than to take the advice they give you in righteousness.

Chapter
10

It's Worth the Effort

The scribes and the Pharisees were the only people Christ couldn't seem to tolerate. He had compassion for other kinds of sinners, but he just couldn't quite take the scribes and the Pharisees because they were such hypocrites. They were always trying to convey the impression, "We keep the commandments, we are righteous, we are living the law"; but they were hypocrites when it came to the spirit of the law.

On one occasion they found fault with the Savior's disciples for eating without ceremonially washing their hands, which to the scribes and Pharisees was required by tradition. Jesus rebuked them for attending to their traditions while neglecting the commandments of God. Their traditions, he reminded them, had invented ways to avoid honoring their parents; for all they had to do was to say "Corban" and they felt themselves relieved of an important aspect of the commandment of God, "Honor thy father and thy mother."

It's too bad, but that's essentially the way it is sometimes when we don't really respect and honor our parents. Sometimes we go out and try to do all sorts of things which in themselves are good and worthwhile — try to be the president of the seminary class, try to become an Eagle Scout, try to be all sorts of things — but we ignore the very things that matter most. And one of the things that matters most is, How do you treat your parents? If you want a barometer on your spiritual maturity, I'd say it would have to be how you treat your parents.

One little boy who wasn't yet in school had been listening to his older brothers and sisters discuss their mathematics. That night as his mother tucked him into bed he looked at her, kissed her goodnight, and said, "Mom, I love you to infinity."

"That's a pretty big word for such a little boy," his mother said. "Do you know what it means?"

"Sure I do, Mom," he replied. "It means I love you on and on forever."

Somehow this child had obtained a sense about eternal things. When we are able to see our parents and family in the light of eternal values, everything changes.

As members of the Lord's church, we don't drink and we don't smoke. We *don't* do a lot of things. But most of these things we don't do aren't really anywhere near as important as how we treat our parents. That doesn't mean that things like breaking the Word of Wisdom aren't important, it's just that this other, positive commandment is so important in comparison. This is the vast, big one — the commandment to honor father and mother.

Now, as we said before, parents come in various sizes, ages, and shapes. They do have their faults, some of which were outlined by John in chapter 2, and maybe your father fits all those things on that list. But as John said about his dad, probably half those things aren't even true about your parents. There are so many good things about them that if you'll look for those good things you'll have no trouble about loving them. Here's the approach you need: "My parents aren't perfect, but I'm going to try to help them to become perfect by loving them and honoring them and telling them how well I think they are doing. I'm going to kneel down as soon as they say it's time for prayer, and if they never say it's time for prayer I'll encourage them to do so. Without preaching to them all the time, and by accepting them the way they are, I'm going to help them be better."

If you feel that your parents are trying to be too good, and are trying to make you be too good, just try to understand why they're doing it. And try to go along with them. I know that sometimes it's difficult. Lifting weights in the weight room is difficult. So is rebuilding a new engine on a car. Everything that is really worthwhile is difficult. So I give you the same advice a judge gave to a sixty-year-old man who had just been sentenced to sixty years in prison. He said to the judge, "Judge, I'm sixty years old. I can't serve sixty years." The judge answered him, "You just do your best." And that's what I say to you. If you really want to help to improve the situation at home, and if you do your best and if you pray for the Lord's help, he will bless you and your best will be good enough.

One of my boys said, "Tell me a story." I responded, "I will, but it's going to be a Bible story." So I told him the story of David and Goliath. At the appropriate point, I said, "The boy got some stones, and he flipped one of them and hit that giant, and the giant fell and David defeated him." Then I asked my son, "How could a young man defeat a giant like that?"

He didn't answer for a minute, so I decided to suggest

the right answer to him. "Was it because Heavenly Father was with him?" I said. He thought for a while and then said, "No, Dad, he didn't need Heavenly Father because he had a sling."

Of course, I ought to have spanked him right on the spot. Sometimes I feel like spanking anybody who thinks they've got such a good personal sling that they don't need the Lord. Let me assure you that you do need the Lord. And almost as much as you need the Lord, you need your parents. In a sense they're your link with the Lord. If you'll do your best to honor them, that's what the Lord expects. When you do that, the benefits will be yours as well as theirs.

My sons play basketball, and under certain situations they shoot foul shots which decide the outcome of the games. I asked one of my sons, "How do you take that pressure?"

"Pressure?" he responded. "Dad, that's not pressure. I'll tell you what's pressure. Pressure is trying to be the kind of son that you deserve."

I had to turn away. I didn't deserve that kind of statement. But it had to be recorded as one of the happiest single moments of my life. Why not give your mom and dad a moment like that right away?

You see, life is made up of moments, for you and for your parents no less than everyone else. Make family moments happy and family life will be happy. So treat your parents in ways such as this book suggests and they, like you, will find their lives improving and their happiness increasing.

And that has everything to do with the art of raising parents.